Look
What
I Found!

In the
Woods

Paul Humphrey

W

FRANKLIN WATTS

LONDON • SYDNEY

This edition 2009

Franklin Watts
338 Euston Road
London NW3 3LD

Franklin Watts Australia
Level 17/207 Kent Street
Sydney, NSW 2000

© Franklin Watts 2005

Planning and production by Discovery Books Limited
Editor: Geoff Barker
Designer: Ian Winton
Natural history consultant: Michael Chinery
Language consultant: Helen Barden
Photographer: Chris Fairclough (including front cover)

Additional photographs: Bruce Coleman: 13 (Colin Varndell),
18 (Robert Maier), 25b (Kim Taylor), 27 (Allan G. Potts);
Corbis: 23b; FLPA: 19 (Tony Hamblin), 23t (Ray Bird).

A CIP catalogue record for this book is available from the
British Library

ISBN 978 0 7496 8912 4

Dewey decimal classification number: 577.3

Printed in China

Franklin Watts is a division of Hachette Children's Books,
an Hachette UK Company.
www.hachette.co.uk

Contents

I went to the woods with
Mum and this is what I found.

There were lots of wild flowers.

They were all sorts of colours.

There were different types
of tree. I felt their bark.

silver birch

oak

One was smooth,
one was bumpy.

I found a tiny tree. It will be
a huge oak tree one day.

Some of the trees had spiky
leaves, like this holly.

Others had cones, like this fir.

I liked the smell of the trees.

I followed a track.

There were
cowslips
everywhere.

I heard a woodpecker
hammering on a tree trunk.

chick

It was looking for insects
to feed to its chick.

13

There were dead trees on
the ground.

fungi

This one had fungi growing on it.

I looked in the grass nearby...

and found this shiny, black beetle.

You can tell how old a tree is by counting the rings from the centre of the trunk.

I lay on the grass...

and saw two flies meet
on a yellow flower.

A mouse was sitting
on a cone.

I looked up and saw a
squirrel looking at me.

Down at the bottom of the trees I saw some fungi.

fungi

Toadstools are fungi too.

I found
a bird's
feather.

Mum and I walked along the
mossy bank of a stream.

A fox had left tracks in the mud.

We saw something move. It was the fox!

Under the tall pine trees was a pile of pine needles and twigs.

It was a wood ants' nest.

Thousands
of ants
lived there!

foxgloves

bracken

I saw foxgloves and bracken.

The sun was starting to set.
I heard an owl hoot.

It was time to go home!

Can you find these in the book?

wild flowers

fox

fungi

28

cone

beetle

ants' nest

Index